HISTORIC DOORWAYS OF SAN ANTONIO

4880 Lower Valley Road Atglen, Pennsylvania 19310

Text and Photography by
Frederick R. Preston, Ed.D.
Foreword by Judge Nelson W. Wolff

Cover: Marion Koogler McNay Art Museum – 1929, Ayres & Ayres, Spanish Mediterranean.

Title page: Mission San José – 1782, Spanish Colonial Baroque. *This is the entrance to the church sacristy.*

Other Schiffer Books on Related Subjects:
Ghosts of San Antonio

Copyright © 2009 by Frederick R. Preston
Library of Congress Control Number: 2008938134

Covers and Book Designed by: Bruce Waters
Type set in Zurich BT

ISBN: 978-0-7643-3167-1
Printed in China

Schiffer Books are available at special discounts for bulk purchases for sales promotions or premiums. Special editions, including personalized covers, corporate imprints, and excerpts can be created in large quantities for special needs. For more information contact the publisher:

Published by Schiffer Publishing Ltd.
4880 Lower Valley Road
Atglen, PA 19310
Phone: (610) 593-1777, Fax: (610) 593-2002
E-mail: Info@schifferbooks.com

For the largest selection of fine reference books on this and related subjects, please visit our web site at **www. schifferbooks.com**
We are always looking for people to write books on new and related subjects. If you have an idea for a book please contact us at the above address.

This book may be purchased from the publisher.
Include $5.00 for shipping.
Please try your bookstore first.
You may write for a free catalog.

In Europe, Schiffer books are distributed by
Bushwood Books
6 Marksbury Ave.
Kew Gardens
Surrey TW9 4JF England
Phone: 44 (0) 20 8392-8585, Fax: 44 (0) 20 8392-9876
E-mail: info@bushwoodbooks.co.uk
Website: www.bushwoodbooks.co.uk
Free postage in the U.K., Europe, air mail at cost.

Contents

Foreword

San Antonio takes great pride in preserving and restoring historic buildings. During my time as a councilman and mayor in the late 80s and early 90s, we passed the nation's strongest preservation ordinance. As mayor, I led the effort to restore the exterior of City Hall, and now as Bexar County Judge, we are in the middle of a ten year plan to restore ten historic courtrooms and the exterior of the Courthouse. Although we protect and preserve, we seldom take the time to carefully observe our historic treasures. On the opposite page, the Alamo City's most famous preserved colonial doors, the "Veramendi doors", is an excellent example of one of these gems.

Sometimes it takes a newcomer to better appreciate the magnificence of the structures that we take for granted. Educator, Dr. Fred Preston, who moved to San Antonio from New York just three years ago, focused on the doorways of our historic treasures. With his passion for photography he proceeded to capture artistic, stunning doorways. When you look at his photographs, you wish you could grab the knob, and walk into a past time when life moved at an elegant and slower pace.

Dr. Preston walked the streets of the King William neighborhood where he photographed the doorways of Greek Revival, Victorian and Italianate architectural designed homes. Most of the original homes were built by German immigrants who first settled in San Antonio in the mid 1850s. Ernst Altgelt was the first to build his home in 1867 at 236 King William. Today, the roughly 22 block neighborhood bordering on the San Antonio River, just south of downtown, has approximately 80 historic structures.

At the turn of the 20th century San Antonio began to expand north. Prosperous citizens built homes in what is now known as the Monte Vista Historic District. Fred Preston's photographs of these doorways lead us back in time to San Antonio's "Gilded Age" from 1890 to 1930. They open into an eclectic mix of grand mansions and smaller homes.

Dr. Preston has also photographed the doorways to many of our public historic buildings. These include the Courthouse, City Hall, and the Missions. Come touch, feel and open these valuable treasures.

Hon. Nelson W. Wolff
Bexar County Judge and
former Mayor of San Antonio
(1991-1995)

Veramendi Palace doors – late 1700s, Spanish Colonial.
Doors on Display at the Alamo Chapel. (opposite)

Acknowledgements

The birth and delivery of this book is the result of the active assistances of several people. To these supporters I extend my forever gratitude.

To Tonia Fite, and my daughter, Lisa, for their love and spiritual empowerment.

To John McKusker, and Ben Brewer for their critique and assessment of my photography as publishable material.

To Suzanne Velázquez, for lending her exceptional editing skills and Vincent Louie for his digital photography editing.

To Milton Guess, Marco Barros and Linda Winchester of the San Antonio Tourism Council, and Laura Garcia at the Alamo for providing strategic referrals in the early stages of my work.

To the Monte Vista Historical Association, particularly Rosanne White, for the exposure in their newsletter, and the architectural background data available on their website.

Sheri Mumme and Oscar Camacho were always there for me offering artistic consultation and assistance on a range of issues associated with this project.

Also, the kind assistance of Elizabeth Standifird and Ron Bauml at the San Antonio Conservation Society, was particularly helpful to my research of data on the featured structures.

Others providing assistance include the San Antonio Downtown Residents Association, and Dr. Richard Bruce Winders, historian and curator at The Alamo.

Finally, special gratitude is due to the many superlative architects whose artistic genius is strategic to the landscape of beautiful architecture present in the Alamo City community. An index of their work is placed at the back of the book.

Introduction

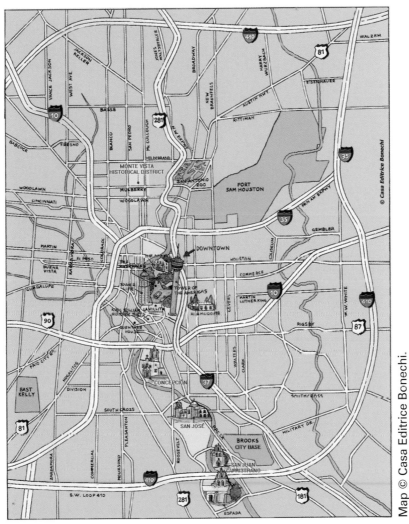

Map © Casa Editrice Bonechi.

Almost universally, entrances or doorways have historically been and continue to be recognized as one of the most significant architectural features of a building. While serving basic functions such as providing passage, ventilation, light, safety, and privacy, doorways also dynamically influence or even shape, the visual aesthetic and emotional impact of a structure. This feature can also serve as a vehicle to introduce, or further, accent social factors such as cultural heritage or economic status.

Made of olive wood, hand-carved and overlaid with gold, the ancient doorways to King Solomon's Temple reflected its role as the primary center for religious worship, as well as, the king's enormous wealth. Likewise, the architectural trend of U.S. doorways very much reflects the socio-economic, political, and cultural demographics during different periods of our history. Commenting on the historical design trend of the typical American home exterior front entrance, Vincente and Connor note that we have gone "from puritanical Colonial to wealthy Georgian, from the pioneering spirit of the western Prairie style to the industrially inspired Modern." (Vincente, Paulo and Tom Connor, *The Language of Doors*. New York: Artisan, 2005.)

The current popularity of eclectic entrance designs is consistent with our nation's rapidly increasing multi-ethnic and multi-cultural populace.

Even with an impressive architectural history, like trees in a forest, the beauty and elegance of doorways can easily go unnoticed and under appreciated by the casual observer. My own attention to this design feature was awakened on a trip to Florence and Rome, Italy over thirty years ago. The entrances to churches, palaces, courtyards, commercial buildings, etc. collectively sparked both an emotional and cognitive appreciation for their significance to the overall exterior grandeur and character of a structure. More recently, viewing San Antonio through the eyes of a relatively new resident has nurtured my desire to share this appreciation of the beauty to be found in exterior doorways, particularly front entrances.

San Antonio, the home of The Alamo, is currently the seventh largest city in the nation. Yet, its architectural charm and beauty, along with its community warmth, contribute to a city ambience that projects the hospitality and fellowship of a neighborhood. Further, at least four characteristics of Alamo City combine to make it a unique architectural landscape for exterior doorways:

1. Its strategic significance to both Texas and United States history,

2. Its successful preservation advocates, such as Adina De Zavala, former San Antonio Mayor Maury Maverick and the San Antonio Conservation Society,

3. Its multi-ethnic and multi-cultural heritage and legacy, and,

4. Its good fortune in benefiting from the contributions of over forty prominent architects in its early growth and development.

The result is a sizeable inventory of well maintained, beautiful architecture represented in twenty-two nationally registered historic districts. Focusing on historic entrances in the downtown commercial area, its immediate adjoining neighborhoods, and the church missions, I have utilized the camera to share the heritage, character, and elegance of the city's diverse architecture.

The book is organized into three chapters that reflect the historical chronology of San Antonio's growth and development. Chapter 1 centers on architecture downtown and in the missions starting from the early 1700s. Chapter 2 covers the King William Historic District structures commencing in the mid 1800s. Chapter 3 focuses on the Monte Vista Historic District homes built in the early 1900s. Intending this book to be a photographic showcase of architecture, I have relied upon the doorway photographs to tell their story with limited narrative. However, to the degree the data was available, each picture is captioned with the building name (current and past), date constructed, architect, and design style. The result, I hope, is a celebration of San Antonio's historical architecture conservation that provides joy to San Antonians, architects, photographers, preservationists, and even those individuals seeking inspiration to restore the doorways of their own home.

Chapter 1

The Missions and Historic Downtown

The founding settlement of San Antonio, early in the 18th century, provided some of the city's most significant architecture. Particularly notable are the four church missions established by Spain along the San Antonio River–Mission San José, Mission Concepcion, Mission San Juan, and Mission Espada. Even more significant, located in the heart of downtown, is the Mission San Antonio de Valero (the Alamo). These restored historic treasures with magnificent doorways, collectively, are the nation's largest grouping of stone Spanish Colonial missions in a city. Likewise, the restored La Villita district, situated four blocks from the Alamo, features Spanish-Mexican vernacular style residential structures, mostly from the mid- to late 1800s. A more substantial residence from the same period is the flat roofed, one-story, plastered stone Spanish Governor's Palace, which housed the captain of the city's "presidio" or fortress.

The rapid influx of American settlers, as well as immigrants from places like Mexico, Germany, and the Canary Islands only a few years after the Battle of the Alamo in 1836, and the arrival of railroad passage in 1877 substantially boosted the city's economy. This economic growth produced impressive commercial and government buildings like the Menger Hotel, Sunset Railroad Station, San Antonio National Bank, City Hall, and the Bexar County Courthouse, the largest historic courthouse in the state of Texas. The design diversity of these structures reflects the city's multi-cultural legacy.

San Antonio's continued status in the early 1900s as Texas's largest city, and its recognition as the trade crossroads of the southwestern United States, provided more commercial architectural gems. Among these structures are the Tower Life, Federal Reserve Bank, and Alamo National Bank buildings. All three buildings feature Neo-classical design, popular nationally at the time. Most other downtown building projects during this period further expanded the city's design diversity. Current alternative use of many of these buildings has successfully sustained the historical architectural integrity. The stunning doors of the Drury Plaza Hotel are a prime example.

Overall, the diversity of beautiful historically significant doorways pictured in this chapter is a testament to San Antonio's inspiring, colorful, and multi-cultural past.

Sunset Station – 1877, John Isaacs, Mission Revival. *Doors on station's rear extension.*

San Fernando Cathedral – 1868, Gothic Revival.

St. Marks Episcopal Church – 1875, Richard Upjohn, Gothic Revival.

Main Plaza Building *(formerly Frost National Bank)* – 1922, Sanquinet & Staats, Greek Revival.

The Maloney Building *(formerly San Antonio First National Bank)* – 1886, Cyrus W. Eidlitz, Moorish.

The Menger Hotel – 1859,
John Fries, Greek Revival.

St. Anthony Hotel – 1909, J. Flood Walker &
John Marriott, Spanish Colonial Revival.

Mission San Antonio de Valero (*the Alamo*) – 1718, Spanish Colonial, *Structure currently referred to as the Alamo was the mission's church building.*

The Drury Hotel *(formerly Alamo National Bank)* – 1929, Graham, Anderson, Probst & White, Beau-Arts Classical Tradition.

The Consulate of Mexico *(formerly Federal Reserve Bank)* – 1928, Ayres & Ayres, Neoclassical.

Tower Life Building *(Smith-Young Tower)* – 1929, Ayres & Ayres, Gothic Revival, *Tallest building in Texas until early 1950s.*

17

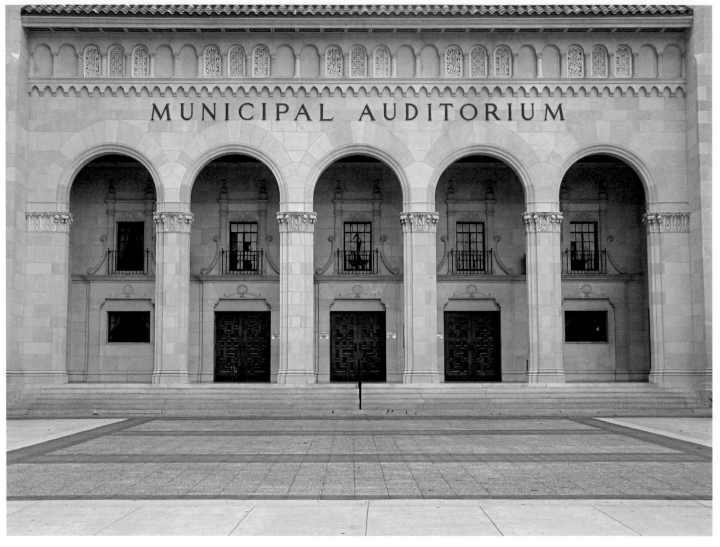

Municipal Auditorium – 1926, Ayres & Ayres, George Willis & E. T. Jackson, Spanish Colonial Revival.

First Baptist Church of San Antonio – 1925, Neoclassical.

Atlee B. Ayres Building – 1911, Atlee B. Ayres, Neoclassical.

Casino Club Building – 1927, Kelwood Co.,
Art Deco with Mayan detail.

Caxias House – c.1855, Spanish Colonial.

Scottish Rite Cathedral – 1922, Hubert M. Greene & Ralph Cameron, Classical Revival. *Currently houses the Masonic library and museum.*

St. Martin House – c.1854, Spanish Colonial.

Southwest School of Art & Craft *(formerly Ursuline Convent & Academy)* – 1851- 1883,
Jules Poinsard, French Gothic Revival & Vernacular Influences.

Spanish Governor's Palace
– c 1749, Spanish Colonial

City Hall – 1891, Otto Kramer, J. Flood Walker & John M. Marriott, European Renaissance Revival.

Express-News Building *(formerly San Antonio Light Building)* – 1931, Mission Revival, *Stone bas relief by Pompeo Coppini.*

Mission San Francisco de la Espada – c. 1745, Spanish Colonial Doorway features irregular Mudejar arch.

Mission San Juan Capistrano – c.1772, Spanish Colonial.

Mission San José – 1782, Spanish Colonial Baroque, *Known as the "Queen of the Missions"*.

Bexar County Courthouse – 1890, James R. Gordon & D. E. Laub, Romanesque Revival.

AT&T Building *(formerly Southwest Bell Building)* – 1931, I. R. Temlin, Spanish Baroque.

Mission Concepcíon – 1755, *One of the nation's oldest original stone churches. (opposite page)*

Sullivan Carriage House – 1886, Alfred Giles, Richardson Romanesque, *Structure
was relocated from downtown to the San Antonio Botanical Garden in 1995.*

Chapter 2
King William Historic District

A 1967 city ordinance enabled the King William Area to become the first Texas neighborhood in 1968 to be designated as a Historic District. Located immediately to the south of downtown and adjacent to La Villita, it is currently roughly bounded by Durango Boulevard, South St. Mary's Street, and the San Antonio River.

The early settlement of the district was very much associated with the entrepreneurial spirit of many of the city's German immigrants in the latter half of the 1800s. Examples of these pioneering individuals include Carl Guenther (miller), Eduard Steves (lumberman), Karl William Groos (banker), Ernst Altgelt (real estate investor), Carl Harnisch (confectioner), and Josiah Pancoast (tailor). They, along with a lesser number of other affluent non-German San Antonians, began building magnificent Victorian, Greek Revival, and Italianate style mansions and cottages in the area. During this period King William quickly became the city's most fashionable and elegant neighborhood.

However, by the 1930s this area had declined and many of the impressive old homes were in disrepair or converted to apartment dwellings. Fortunately, the 1950s witnessed the onset of the attraction of young professionals to the district and many of them valued its close proximity to downtown. This demographic trend, as well as the energetic efforts of the King William and San Antonio Conservation Societies, led to the restoration of many of its historically significant homes. Today, as a part of a larger trendy arts area that includes the "Southtown" commercial corridor and the Lavaca and Blue Star communities, the King William District is again a fashionable community with elegant homes and doorways giving pleasure to hordes of tourist and photographic opportunities for this book.

Josiah Pancoast Cottage – 1900, Victorian Cottage.

Casbeers at the Church *(formerly Alamo Methodist Church)* – 1913, Beverly W. Spillman, Spanish Mission Colonial Revival.

Gething House – 1891, Neoclassical.

Carl Wilhelm August Groos House – 1880, Alfred Giles, Italian Villa.

Josiah Pancoast House – 1878, Classical Revival.

M. L. Oppenheimer House – 1900, Richardson Romanesque Revival.

Stevens/James House – 1881, Italianate.

Abbott Homestead – 1889, Queen Anne.

Lassner/Gallagher House – 1893, Neoclassical.

35

LaCroix / Goldschmidt
House – 1888, Folk Victorian.

Witte / Garza House – 1903, Spanish Revival.

Haarmann/Goeth House – 1893,
Romanesque.

George Kalteyer House – 1892, James Riely
Gordon, Richardsonian Romanesque.

S. J. Brookes House – 1890, Queen Anne.

Alexander Joske House – 1900, S. L. McAdoo, Colonial Revival.

Ike West House – 1887, Victorian Second Empire.

Chabot House – 1875, Gothic Revival.

Gustav Groos House – 1875, Victorian Gothic.

Paul Meerscheidt/Davis House – 1888-89, Neoclassical.

41

Ernst Schuchard House – 1927,
Kurt Beckmann, Neoclassical.

c.1940s, Art Moderne.

Ernst Altgelt House – 1878, Victorian.

1877, Alfred Giles, Italianate.

Carl Harnisch House – 1884, Queen Anne.

Steves Homestead – 1876, Alfred Giles, Victorian French Second Empire.

Henry Boerner House –
1915, Neoclassical.

1st Ernst Altgelt House – 1866, Neoclassical.

Van Derlip House – c.1872, Classical Revival.

Adolph Heusinger House – 1885, Italianate.

Kohler House – 1903, Atlee B. Ayres, Neoclassical.

Ellis-Meusebach House – 1884, Victorian Folk Cottage.

Adolph Wagner House – 1885, Victorian Cottage.

Albert Steves House – 1883, Alfred Giles, Italian Villa.

Anton Wulff House – 1870, Italianate Villa.

1906, Queen Anne with Romanesque doorway.

Mitchell-Oge House – 1857/1882, Alfred Giles, Greek Revival.

51

Chapter 3

Monte Vista Historic District

A walk or drive around the Monte Vista residential neighborhood frequently evokes comments such as prosperous, well preserved, inviting, diverse, and stunning. Its extensive stock of vintage homes is complimented by gorgeous tree-lined avenues, boulevards and parkways. Alleys located behind the houses provide utilitarian access for trash collection and sighting for utility poles, further enhancing the uncluttered visual charm of the streets. This author has often referred to the district as an architectural *tour de force* of well-maintained, eclectic, and awesomely beautiful 19th and 20th century residences featuring a broad range of eye-catching front entrances.

One of the nations largest nationally registered historic districts, Monte Vista covers 100 city blocks with approximately 1500 homes. Most of these structures were built during the San Antonio economic growth period between 1890 and the late 1920s. Situated on hilly terrain elevated approximately 100 feet above and one-and-a-half miles north of downtown San Antonio, the neighborhood is an example of early suburban growth spurred by the expansion of streetcar and automobile transportation.

Though early residents of the Monte Vista District were real estate investors, oil-rich entrepreneurs, and wealthy cattlemen, they were soon followed by other professionals and trades persons with more modest incomes. As a result, grand mansions "coexist with more modest vernacular dwellings, bungalows, and apartment houses…" (Pfeiffer, Maria Watson and Sue Ann Pemberton-Haugh [prepared by]. *Monte Vista Historic District, National Register of Historic Places Registration Form*. 1998, p. 11.)

Over twenty prominent architects, such as Adams & Adams, Ayres & Ayres, Beverley W. Spillman, and the Kelwood Co., contributed to the execution of over forty different architectural styles visible in Monte Vista. Among the designs current are Spanish Colonial Revival, Classical Revival, Craftsman, Greek Revival, Italianate, Mediterranean, Prairie, Tutor, Spanish Eclectic, and Gothic. The chapter showcases 115 beautiful doorways from this large gallery of impressive residences.

1921, Smith & Kelly, Italian Renaissance.

1930, Robert McGarraugh, Spanish Eclectic.

1920, Italian Renaissance.

1930, Spanish Colonial Revival.

1924, Colonial Revival.

1929, Robert B. Kelly, Tudor.

1906, Colonial Revival.

c.1929, Neoclassical.

1928, Spanish Eclectic.

1924, Ayres & Ayres, Spanish Colonial Revival.

1927, Frost Carvel, Spanish Eclectic.

P. J. McNeel House – 1925, Kelwood Co., Spanish Colonial Revival.

1925, Ayres & Ayres, Spanish Colonial Revival.

1928, Frost Carvel, Tudor.

1923, Ayres & Ayres, Spanish Colonial Revival.

c.1920, Craftsman.

Paul Adams House – 1924, Adams & Adams,
Colonial Revival.

1929, Spanish Eclectic.

1920, Craftsman and Spanish Eclectic.

c.1923, Tudor.

1924, Prairie.

1925, Colonial Revival – Dutch.

1928, Glenn C. Wilson, Italian Renaissance.

1924, Ayres & Ayres, Colonial Revival.

Albert Prucha House – 1928, John M. Marriott, Spanish Colonial Revival. (Opposite page)

Julius Seligman House – 1926, Kelwood Co., Italian Villa.

1921, Mrs. Martin Wright, Spanish Eclectic.

1927, Robert McGarraugh, Spanish Colonial Revival.

Herbert L. Kokernot House – 1928, Russell Brown, Spanish Colonial Revival.

1928, Albaugh & Steinboner, Tudor.

c.1935, Tudor.

c.1929, Tudor.

1924, Neoclassical.

c.1920, Craftsman.

1919, Craftsman updated with Mexican entrance.

1912, H. A. Reuter, Neoclassical.

1926, Italian Renaissance.

1928, Tudor.

1924, Frost Carvel, Spanish Colonial Revival.

1930, Spanish Eclectic.

1928, Beverly W. Spillman, Tudor.

1920, Tudor.

1927, Colonial Revival.

1922, Ernest Scrivener, Italian Renaissance.

1927, Ayres & Ayres, Spanish Colonial Revival.

c.1925, Spanish Colonial Revival.

1925, Robert McGarraugh, Spanish Colonial Revival.

c.1925, Spanish Colonial Revival.

c.1925, Colonial Revival.

1927, Kelwood Co., Spanish Colonial Revival.

1926, Robert B. Kelly, Italian Renaissance.

1920, Ralph H. Cameron, Italian Renaissance.

1922, Atlee B. Ayres, Spanish Colonial Revival with Byzantine Doorway arch.

c.1925, Spanish Colonial Revival.

1926, Kelwood Co., Spanish Colonial Revival.

c.1925, Tudor.

1909, Shingle.

c.1925, Colonial Revival.

1928, Kelwood Co., Spanish Colonial Revival.

1925, L. Harrington, Neoclassical.

1906/1925, Atlee B. Ayres, Neoclassical.

1925, Frost Carvel, Spanish Colonial Revival.

1923, Adams & Adams, Spanish Colonial Revival.

1930, French Eclectic.

1929, Tudor.

1927, James L. White, Spanish Colonial Revival.

1928, Colonial Revival.

c.1930, Clemens Fridell, Tudor.

1921, Emmet T. Jackson, Craftsman.

1905/1912, Carleton W. Adams, Craftsman.

c.1925, Craftsman.

c.1925, Spanish Eclectic.

1921, Colonial Revival.

1933, N. Straus Nayfach, French Eclectic.

1922, Henry Phelps, Italian Renaissance.

c.1925, Spanish Colonial Revival (Opposite page)

c.1920, Italian Renaissance.

D. K. Furnish House – 1903, Ayres & Ayres, Mission Revival.

1929, Ralph H. Cameron, Spanish Colonial Revival.

Mary A. Stowers House – 1925, Adams & Adams, Italian Renaissance Revival.

1930, Will N. Noonan, Spanish Colonial Revival.

c.1925, Tudor.

1921, Tudor.

J. S. Sweeney House – 1924, Adams & Adams, Neoclassical.

1918, Smith & Kelly, Colonial Revival.

1928, Harvey P. Smith, Spanish Colonial Revival.

1924, Kelwood Co., Spanish Eclectic

John M. Marriott House – 1926, John M. Marriott, Spanish Colonial Revival.

Louis Kayton House – 1928, Richard Van Patten, Tudor.

Fred Hornaday House – 1929, Ralph H. Cameron, Colonial Revival. *Features broken-pediment Palladian entrance.*

Frederick J. Combs House – 1922, Russell Brown, Tudor.

1927, Robert McGarraugh, Tudor.

Theodore Plummer House – 1927, Richard Vander Stratten, Italian Renaissance. *Features lunette by Hannibal Pianta.*

1925, Will N. Noonan, Colonial Revival – Dutch.

1924, Harvey P. Smith, Spanish Colonial Revival.

1918, Atlee B. Ayres, Colonial Revival.

1917, H. A. Reuter, Italian Renaissance.

Douglas Skinner House – 1929, Harvey P. Smith, Tudor.

1921, Atlee B. Ayres, Italian Renaissance.

1912, Reuter & Harrington, Tudor.

Charles Baumberger House – 1929, Adams & Adams, Spanish Colonial Revival.

Wallace Rogers House – 1923, Adams & Adams, Italian Renaissance Revival.

Jack R. Locke House – 1928, Richard
Vander Stratten, Spanish Colonial Revival.

c.1929, Tudor.

Edward N. Requa Rent House – 1922, C. B. Schoeppl, Colonial Revival.

1928, Spanish Colonial Revival.

c.1925, Atlee B. Ayres, Italian Renaissance.

Beecher F. Stout House – 1925, Kelwood Co., Tudor.

c.1920, Craftsman.

1930, Ayres & Ayres,
Spanish Eclectic.

1927, Robert McGarraugh, Spanish Eclectic.

1926, Thomson & Swaine, Spanish Colonial Revival.

1928, Spanish Colonial Revival.

References

Introduction

Fisher, Lewis. *Saving San Antonio: The Precarious Preservation of a Heritage*. Lubbock, Texas: Texas Tech University Press, 1996.

Jennings, Frank W. *San Antonio: The Story of an Enchanted City*. Austin, Texas: Eakin Press, 2002.

Oussani, Solomon G. *The Catholic Encyclopedia*, Vol. 14. New York: Robert Appleton Co., 1912.

Vincente, Paulo and Tom Connor. *The Language of Doors.* New York: Artisan, 2005.

Temple of Solomon, The Jewish Encyclopedia. New York: Funk & Wagnalls, 1906.

Chapter 1

Christian, Ralph J. (prepared by). *La Villita, National Register of Historic Places Nomination Form*. Historic Landmarks Project, 1979.

City of San Antonio, Downtown Operations Dept. *La Villita A History.* No date.

Cooke, Stephanie Hetos and Amy E. Dase (prepared by). *Smith-Young Tower, San Antonio, TX., National Register of Historic Places, Registration Form.* Texas Historical Commission, 1990.

Hemphill, Hugh. *The Railroads of San Antonio and South Central Texas*. San Antonio, Texas: Maverick Publishing Co., 2006.

Jennings, Frank W. *San Antonio: The Story of an Enchanted City*. Austin, Texas: Eakin Press, 2002.

Smith, Stephen and Joe R. Williams (prepared by). *Southern Pacific Railroad Passenger Station, National Register of Historic Places, Inventory - Nomination Form.* Texas Historical Commission, 1975.

Texas State Historical Association and University of Texas at Austin. *Handbook of Texas Online.* 1999. Accessed 2008 (http://www.tshaonline.org/handbook/online/).

Williams, Dana Schultz. *The History and the Mystery of the Menger Hotel.* Plano, Texas: Republic of Texas Press, 2000.

Chapter 2

Burkholder, Mary V. *Down the Acequia Madre: In the King William Historic District.* San Antonio, Texas: privately printed, 1976.

Burkholder, Mary V. *The King William Area: A History and a Guide to the Houses.* San Antonio, Texas: The King William Association, 1973.

Garner, John C. (prepared by). *Juliana C. Van Derlip House.* Historic American Buildings Survey, 1969.

Jennings, Frank W. *San Antonio: The Story of an Enchanted City*. Austin, Texas: Eakin Press, 2002.

King William Association. *King William Historic District.* Accessed 2008 (http://kingwilliamassociation.org/joomla/).

Lumsden, Sharmyn (prepared by). *Alamo Methodist Church, National Register of Historic Places, Nomination Form*. Texas Historical Commission, 1979.

Texas Historical Commission. *King William Historic District*. Texas Historic Sites Atlas Online (http://atlas.thc.state.tx.us/).

The City of San Antonio Historic Preservation. *King William Historic District.* Accessed 2008 (http://epay.sanantonio.gov/historic/hddetail.aspx?id=8870).

Chapter 3

Everett, Donald E. *San Antonio's Monte Vista: Architecture and Society in a Guided Age 1890 – 1930,* San Antonio, Texas: Maverick Publishing Co., 1999.

Monte Vista Historical Association. *Monte Vista History.* Accessed 2008 (http://www.montevista-sa.org/).

Pfeiffer, Maria Watson and Sue Ann Pemberton-Haugh (prepared by). *Monte Vista Historic District, National Register of Historic Places Registration Form*. 1998.

Index of Architects

General Index